MOUNT RAINIER
NATIONAL PARK

by

RON WARFIELD

SIERRA PRESS
MARIPOSA, CA

DEDICATION

For my father, John Henry Warfield, who first brought me to Mount Rainier. His joy in being here keeps me warm every time I see The Mountain. —R.W.

ACKNOWLEDGMENTS

Thanks to Jeff Nicholas and Sierra Press for entrusting me to write about my favorite mountain and to Nicky Leach for molding my enthusiasm into meaningful English. Thanks also to Lee Taylor, Sandi Kinzer, Tom Sission, Sheri Forbes, Kevin Bacher, Patti Wold, and Carl Fabiani of Mount Rainier National Park for checking the manuscript for accuracy. Special thanks to Beckie Warfield for decades of encouragement and support. Her ideas and artist's eye reflect in all my work. —R.W.

INSIDE FRONT COVER
The Mountain reflected in a pool near Pinnacle Peak. PHOTO ©LARRY CARVER
PAGE 2
South face of Mount Rainier, sunrise.
PHOTO ©CHARLES GURCHE
TITLE PAGE
Tumtum Peak, winter sunset.
PHOTO ©RON WARFIELD
PAGE 4 (BELOW)
Asters in the fog near Paradise.
PHOTO ©LAURENCE PARENT
PAGE 4/5
Late afternoon light on Mount Rainier, winter on Mazama Ridge. PHOTO ©ALAN MAJCHROWICZ

CONTENTS

PAGE 6/7
Early-morning fog in Stevens Canyon.
PHOTO ©LARRY ULRICH
PAGE 7 (BELOW)
Old growth in the Carbon River Rain Forest.
PHOTO©FRED HIRSCHMANN

THE MOUNTAIN

The swift-flowing Paradise River.

When the majestic Cascade Mountains arose, natural forces bestowed the Mount Rainier region with the best scenic treasures in the Pacific Northwest. The icy dome of 14,410-foot Mount Rainier stands in the middle of it all. This enormous composite volcano projects nearly two vertical miles above a sea of coniferous forest. Seen from a distance, The Mountain looks like a gigantic sun-bleached tree stump. Often cloaked in a stole of clouds, Mount Rainier seems to make its own weather. Up close, it is a wondrous world unto itself. Northwesterners live close to many mountains, but, to everyone who sees it, this is THE Mountain.

Old-growth temperate coniferous forest sweeps down from about 6000 feet on the flanks of The Mountain—forming an emerald setting for the exquisitely rough diamond that is Mount Rainier. The most luxuriant flowers to be found anywhere lie in a subalpine ring sandwiched between dense lower forest and ice on the upper mountain. Benign beauty of the noble mountain belies its tremendous potential to be the most destructive volcano in America.

My father brought me to Mount Rainier five decades ago because he thought it important that I learn firsthand what America's best idea (the National Park Service) is all about. In this paradise, I feel at peace with the world. Like all lovers of mountains, my heart still leaps when I see it. The more I learn about this magical place the more I discover myself. I've figured out that in saving it we become immortal.

Today, first-time visitor Herm and I seek the essence of this place. We're retracing the route of 19th-century explorers and climbers. Their foresight—to save this mountain and its surroundings as the nation's fifth national park on March 2, 1899—made it possible to wander in this wilderness wonderland today.

The best way to learn a place is to follow its rivers. On our approach to The Mountain, we travel up the Nisqually Valley to the river's source at the snout of the Nisqually Glacier on Mount Rainier. We are exploring part of the 90-mile Wonderland Trail that circles The Mountain. As we stroll through some of the last remaining old-growth forest, all is quiet, save for the gentle drips from a thousand branch tips and the melodious calls of birds.

Gossamer clouds scrape the tops of the giant trees. After soaking in drizzle for days, I'm determined that today will be Herm's day to glimpse The Mountain. We exalt in a green cathedral whose walls are colonnades of deeply furrowed Douglas-fir boles, darkly accented by straight-beamed western hemlock and buttress-based western redcedar. The canopy, more than one hundred feet overhead, festooned with lichens and mosses, supports a thriving community of feathered, furry, and slimy creatures that would not feel at home anywhere else. In reverence for the place, we move slowly and quietly among forest friends. I'm glad that The Mountain is not yet visible. On a sunny day, we might blast through this ancient forest masterpiece in our rush to join throngs of mountain worshippers. The joyous

Mount Rainier in autumn. PHOTO ©CHARLES GURCHE

song of the winter wren reminds me that every day is a symphony in the forest primeval.

At the confluence of the Paradise River, we scurry across the Nisqually on a single log bridge, only a few feet above the churning glacier-milk stream. The river is noisily rearranging a levee of luggage trunk-sized boulders recently deposited by a debris flow. Chocolate-colored waters of the glacier-fed Nisqually contrast sharply with the clear snowmelt waters of the Paradise River. As we approach Carter Falls, a water ouzel curtsies on a rock, then dives into the cold spray. Herm spots the nest behind the falls as the slate gray bird delivers a caddis-fly larva to its young.

At Narada Falls, we marvel at the play of intensely colored rainbows across the face of this splendid cascade. When spray envelops us and catches our shadows in a circular rainbow, we become angels in the mist.

During the "sun break," I sneak glances overhead. We're near the top of a thin cloud layer that has obscured The Mountain and the jagged Tatoosh Range summits. If there were no Mount Rainier to steal the scene, the Tatoosh Range would rate national park status, so first-time visitors arriving during one of The Mountain's "moody" periods often ask Herm's innocent question: "Which one is Mount Rainier?"

"Let's get going, I want to check out the meadows," I respond in anticipation of the ultimate view. After a sojourn spent enjoying the serenity at Reflection Lakes, we make our way toward the spine of Mazama Ridge. On this first week of August, the height of the flower season, we revel, waist deep, in extravagantly beautiful floral displays. Naturalist John Muir declared that this was the richest subalpine garden he had ever found. We entirely agree! Scattered atolls of subalpine fir and mountain hemlock frame every view in this perfect floral Paradise.

As Herm and I tramp higher, leaving the trees behind, the flowers brighten in brilliant sunshine. We're floating above the sea of clouds on a fragrant carpet of lupine. In front of us, Mount Rainier towers almost 9000 feet above our flower-filled vantage point. The glaciers cascading from its icy crown add a regal touch to its otherworldly appearance. We stand in awed silence before its magnificence. Then normally dispassionate Herm exclaims, "Wow, it really is THE Mountain!"

Narada Falls on the Paradise River. PHOTO ©CHARLES GURCHE

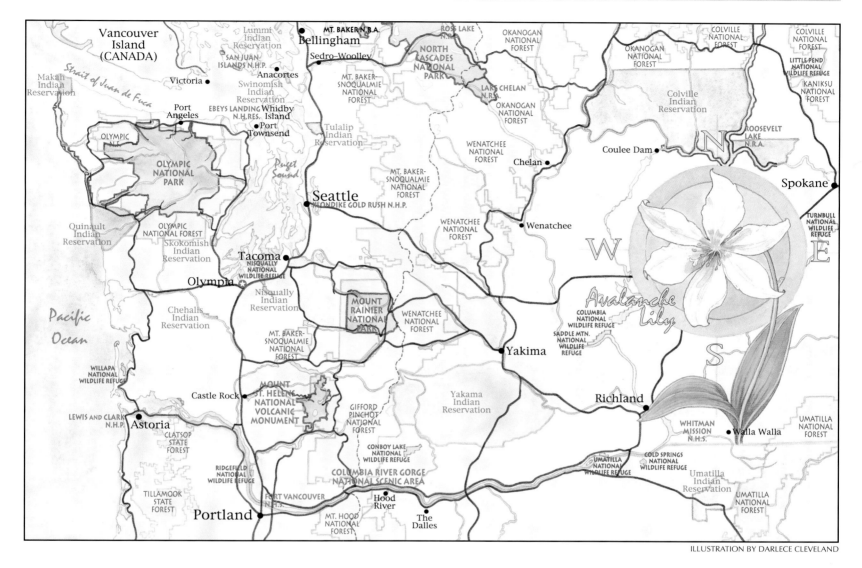

ILLUSTRATION BY DARLECE CLEVELAND

Located just west of the crest of the southern Washington Cascades, Mount Rainier National Park is often described as "an arctic island in a temperate zone." The park preserves a fragment of forested wilderness that only a century ago extended all the way to the shores of Puget Sound. In every direction, from the Columbia River Gorge to the North Cascades, and the Cascade Crest to the Pacific shore, Northwesterners enjoy an abundance of wildland recreational opportunities. For lovers of big old trees and snow-covered mountains, **this is the place.** In a land of superlatives, Mount Rainier sets the standard by which we measure all other mountains.

Visible from the Puget Sound lowlands, Mount Rainier appears to float like an ethereal cloud only a short journey beyond the foothills of the Western Cascades. On sunny days travelers on Interstate 5 between Portland and Seattle de-tour toward this glacier-clad magnet. The Mountain looks so close to Tacoma and Olympia, that visitors are surprised when the round-trip excursion takes all day. Though muddy trails through the ancient forest wilderness have become paved highways, it still takes patience to negotiate the route to Mount Rainier. Too many first-time visitors take a cursory look at the regional map and try to combine visits to The Mountain and Mount St. Helens, only to suffer frustration by sensory overload and gluteal exhaustion from a marathon drive. To these harried park life-listers, I plead: slow down and inhale the fragrance of the forest, or revel in the perfume of a flower-filled meadow. Save other mountains for another day. Wander here for a lifetime if you can.

Travelers searching for variations on the Pacific Northwest theme find nearby national parks and forests rewarding. South of the park, wilderness areas such as Goat Rocks and Mount Adams in the Gifford Pinchot National Forest challenge hikers to explore fascinating volcanic landscapes. William O. Douglas and Norse Peak wilderness areas in the Wenatchee National Forest offer solitude along the park's eastern boundary. Hikers in the Clearwater, Glacier View, and Tatoosh wilderness areas adjacent to the park gain exciting views of Mount Rainier from unfamiliar vantage points. All these areas buffer the park from the increasing pressures of human development. On a grander scale, Mount St. Helens National Volcanic Monument offers an up-close experience of active volcanism. Only a half-day's drive from Mount Rainier, Olympic National Park provides outstanding seacoast, old-growth forest, and mountain top recreation experiences.

Anyone approaching Mount Rainier before about 13,500 years ago would have arrived with cold feet. Glacial ice had covered the Puget Sound lowlands west of The Mountain for thousands of years. No one was here to notice. Small groups may have arrived as early as about 8500 years ago in search of mountain goats and small game. Early no-madic foragers adapted to glacial episodes, volcanism, landslides and lahars, and forest encroachment during the warm period about 8500–4500 years ago.

When too many people competed for limited resources in too little space, nomadic foragers became mass harvesters and storers of lowland resources—mainly salmon.

Later, men hunted elk, deer, mountain goats, and marmots in the subalpine meadows, while women and children collected huckleberries near the forest fringe. When the hunting and berrying sea-son was over, people lit fires to in-crease huckleberry production. Then they returned to established lowland villages east and west of The Mountain.

The existing archaeological record shows that Mount Rainier was not a remote, uninhabited wasteland. More than a focal point of spiri-tual reverence or site for personal vision quests, The Mountain remained linked to people's daily lives by providing food and other resources.

For generations, people made annual migrations to The Mountain. Each group had their own name for the peak. Klickitats and Yakamas, who crossed the Cascades from the east to summer in Yakima Park and the Ohanapecosh Valley, called it Tahoma. Taidnapams, who traveled up the Cowlitz and Ohanapecosh rivers into the Tatoosh

Range, named it Takhoma. Muckleshoots traveled up the Carbon and White river drainages toward Tacobet. Nisqually and Puyallup people, who lived near Puget Sound, followed their eponymous streams to Tacobud, "the place where water comes from."

Traditions and names began a dras-

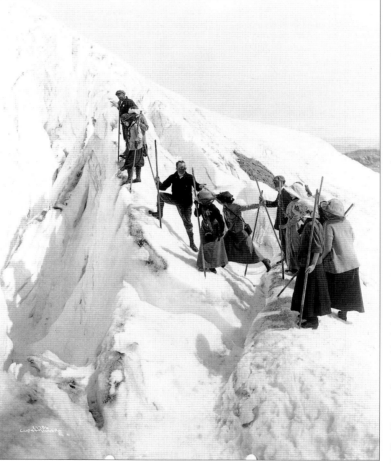

tic change in May 1792 when Captain George Vancouver on His Britannic Majesty's sloop Discovery saw the "very remarkable high, round mountain, covered with snow." He named The Mountain on May 8, 1792, not for its appearance, but for his seafaring friend, Rear Admiral Peter Rainier.

Forty years later, the Hudsons Bay Company set up a trading post at the mouth of the Nisqually River. One of the company, Doctor William Fraser Tolmie, became the first European to enter what is now Mount Rainier National Park, in August 1833.

In 1853, James Longmire led a party of immigrants over Naches Pass northeast of The Mountain and arrived at Fort Nisqually. Longmire and Sluiskin, a Yakama/Taidnapam, assisted Hazard Stevens and Philemon B. Van Trump when they made the first fully documented summit of Mount Rainier, in August 1870.

Longmire returned in 1883 to climb with a party led by P. B. Van Trump. On their return, a stray horse caused the party to discover a lush meadow and mineral springs at the foot of The Mountain. Longmire returned a year later to establish a resort spa. Naturalist John Muir stayed at Longmire's re-sort in August 1888, when he came to climb The Mountain.

Native views of The Moun-tain as provider and source of spiri-tual strength were soon trans-formed into mythology that fo-cused on celebrating The Mountain. Climbers like Van Trump and Fay Fuller, the first woman to summit in 1890, supported Muir's and ge-ologist Bailey Willis' suggestion that Mount Rainier be preserved as a national park to protect its wild scenery for its own sake and to re-serve its features for scientific study. To them, the beauty of The Moun-tain belonged to all people and all future gen-erations, for "the pleasure and instruction of the people." The park was finally established when President William McKinley signed the Mount Rainier National Park bill on March 2, 1899.

The Northern Pacific Railway and the Tacoma Eastern Railroad soon linked the burgeoning cities of Seattle and Tacoma with Washington State's greatest attraction. When established, only one road entered the park—the Mountain Road built by James Longmire to his Longmire Springs Resort. The first day-

ABOVE: Group of men and women climbing Paradise Glacier, circa 1911–1920. PHOTO by CURTIS & MILLER. Courtesy Library of Congress

visitors arrived in 1904 on a Tacoma Eastern Railway excursion train and stage. Only a few years later, convoys of automobiles motored up the road. In 1908, the park became the first in the country to permit automobiles. In 1911, President William Howard Taft rode to Paradise in a car, although mules assisted by towing the car part of the way. Eugene Ricksecker designed the splendid road to be a pleasing drive in harmony with the landscape. Ricksecker's idea that a 100-mile road encircle the mountain was never built, due partly to conservationists' objections, two world wars, and a depression. Instead, the Wonderland Trail, blazed by The Mountaineers in 1915, offers hikers a similar route through the wilderness.

Early park managers dealt with making the park accessible and protecting it from trespass and vandalism. Local entrepreneurs took advantage of "scenic nationalism" to develop accommodations in scenic settings to serve various classes of visitors. In 1916, the newly formed National Park Service consolidated all concession facilities in the park under Rainier National Park Company, which immediately began construction of Paradise Inn. After 1918, new roads, trails, buildings and other "improvements" in the park were required to harmonize with the landscape. In 1924, Mount Rainier National Park hired its first naturalist, Floyd Schmoe, to teach the public about the history and environment of the park.

Between 1916 and 1929, the park was "under construction." Landscape architects controlled construction of facilities and produced Master Plans for the park—the first in the nation. These plans designated where development would occur and where zones would be left undeveloped, as wilderness. During the Depression of the 1930s, major construction continued alongside emergency work relief and national renewal programs of the Public Works Administration (PWA), Works Progress Administration (WPA), and the Civilian Conservation Corps (CCC).

World War II curtailed funding for

construction and public works projects. The park hosted military ski troops, trainees, and families and remained a symbol of the best values for which the nation was fighting. After the war, vacationers overwhelmed the park while facilities, roads, trails, and campgrounds fell into disrepair. In reaction, Mount Rainier became the pilot park for the Mission 66 program, which sought to modernize facilities without impairing their scenic, natural, or historic values. Under Mission 66 park headquarters was relocated outside the park, the Stevens Canyon Road linked Paradise with Sunrise and Ohanapecosh on the park's east side, a new day-use building was constructed at Paradise, and a new visitor cen-

ter was built at Ohanapecosh. Older structures at Paradise were removed, and plans for replacing Paradise Inn were drawn up. Passage of the National Historic Preservation Act in 1966 gave local interests support to save Paradise Inn as a charming reminder of the park's early years.

In recent decades, use patterns and social values have shifted toward natural and historic nostalgia. Wilderness protection and the scientific basis for natural and historic resource management strengthened with the designation of 97 percent of the park as wilderness in 1988. In 1997, Congress designated the 3 percent not preserved in wilderness as a National Historic Landmark District. The developed areas, road system with its bridges, and historic 90-mile Wonderland Trail, backcountry cabins, and fire lookouts remain as the most complete example of 20th-century National Park Service master planning in the nation.

As we enter the 21st century, Mount Rainier retains its links with the Northwest lifestyles and regional identities of Seattle and Tacoma. The National Park Service monitors and manages threats to the park's resources and is restoring damaged areas. As the park becomes more isolated in a sea of modern urbanization, Mount Rainier remains above the fray, providing respite from the region's fast-growing cities. The Mountain has become a part of us all. When we enjoy its resources and preserve its values, we become more human.

About 170 million years ago, while Jurassic dinosaurs roamed, North America broke and headed west from its supercontinent, Pangaea. Then, for millions of years, the Pacific Plate carried chunks of continental material eastward, smearing two mini-continents onto western North America.

About 43 million years ago, the Pacific Plate abruptly swerved northwestward. The Kula Plate squeezed northward between the Pacific and North American plates, thrust beneath (subducted) Alaska, and was replaced by the Farallon Plate. The new plate buckled the edge of the continent as it slid under North America, forming a trough just off the coastline that gathered sediment from coastal swamps. A line of volcanoes erupted along the trough, filling the trough with volcanic debris. Vegetation in the swamps compacted into coal. Resulting beds of sandstones, shales and coal now compose the three-mile-thick Puget Group west of the park.

When volcanoes erupted underwater, steam explosions shattered the lava. The resulting volcanic mud, sand, and sharp-edged pebbles compressed into grayish-green sandstone and breccia layers of the Ohanapecosh Formation.

For 22 million years, volcanoes spewed clouds of ash while glowing avalanches and pyroclastic flows buried landscapes. When the pyroclastic flows came to rest, the remaining heat remelted the ash and pumice to form gray, hard, welded tuff. Jagged remnants of this Stevens Ridge Formation stand as pinnacles and ridges of the Tatoosh Range. Low silica, fluid basalt, and

more viscous, intermediate silica andesite lava flows of later volcanoes spread out over the landscape forming cliffs and summits of the Fifes Peak Formation in the northwestern part of the park.

About 12 million years ago, the subduction rate of the Juan de Fuca Plate (a remnant of the old Farallon plate) increased. Masses of magma (underground molten rock) pushed upwards through the Puget

Group and younger rocks, and hardened beneath the surface to form plutons (large bodies of congealed magma). Salt-and-pepper granodiorite (granite low in quartz) in the Tatoosh Pluton underlies the Tatoosh Range and composes the platform under Mount Rainier. Shortly after the granodiorite congealed, the whole Cascade Range began to rise.

Global climate cooled about 2 million years ago as Pleistocene ice ages shrouded the northern half of North America. Even before a lobe of the Cordilleran ice sheet covered the Puget Sound lowlands under 1000 meters of ice, alpine glaciers formed in the Cascades. Glaciers removed most of the

rock layers covering the Tatoosh Pluton and carved the landscape into horn-shaped peaks, knife-edge ridges, and deep u-shaped valleys. An ancestral volcano rose on the future site of Mount Rainier about 2 million years ago. Though it erupted explosively for nearly a million years, Rainier's ancestor was eventually demolished by the relentless carving of ice.

Before Pleistocene glaciers declared erosional victory over volcanic mountain building, about 500,000 years ago, a new steep-sided stratovolcano, Mount Rainier, melted and blasted its way onto the ice-covered landscape. Multiple lava flows spread across the landscape between thick valley-filling glaciers. Many of the larger lava flows partly melted into the sides of the adjacent glaciers which, in turn, buttressed the lava, allowing the lava to accumulate to remarkable thicknesses, such as the 1200 foot-thick lava flow that underlies Sunrise and Burroughs Mountain, and similarly thick lava flows that support Old Desolate and Grand Park. Meanwhile, repeated explosive eruptions of scoria, ash, and lava blocks formed pyroclastic flows that avalanched down the slopes of the growing cone, piling up into large aprons of rock debris at the volcano's foot. Later glacial erosion carved these into great wedges like Steamboat Prow.

Lava flows comprise about 90 percent of The Mountain's modern cone, but pyroclastic flows of shattered lava also make up a significant portion of the structure. Mount Rainier exploded about 380,000 years ago, ejecting a cloud of glassy, gas-filled pumiceous ash. Later, a more effusive phase of magma eruptions began as large flows coursed down the east and west flanks of the cone. Radial dikes, intruding sheets of magma, fed these flows and exposed surrounding rocks to fierce hydrothermal alteration. Over time, hot acidic water decomposed hard andesite rocks into soft claylike materials susceptible to collapse. Hundreds of small lava flows continued to build Mount Rainier's upper cone. A large explosive eruption about 194,000 years ago formed a 100-foot layer of pumice now exposed in the face of Sunset Amphitheater. For 60,000 years, dike-fed eruptions built the oblong protrusion on The Mountain's east flank— Little Tahoma. Other massive flows formed Ptarmigan, Curtis, and Emerald ridges.

After belching a hot block-and-ash flow that welded into cliffs at Pearl Falls, The Mountain poured a viscous, high-silica, dacite lava flow down Mazama Ridge. Quenched by the Paradise Glacier that occupied Stevens Canyon, the flow remains as a bench perched on the valley wall. Lava flows began erupting from the volcano's upper South face about 40,000 years ago. One flow, confined by glaciers, traveled down a ridge to cap Ricksecker Point, while others terminated higher.

By the time of the last Pleistocene glacial retreat, 12–10,000 years ago, The Mountain's ice-covered summit reached an altitude of more than 15,000 feet. Glaciers had sculpted and shaped the cone, leaving resistant rock cleavers between ice streams.

The Mountain continued to eject intermittent plumes of ash and pyroclastic flows that generated numerous lahars (vol-canic mudflows). About 5,600 years ago, one of these explosive events triggered the collapse of the summit, along with decayed rock that transformed into one of the world's largest mudflows, the Osceola. As the avalanche plummeted over Steamboat Prow, one wave of material coursed down the Emmons Glacier removing the flank between the Prow and Disappointment Cleaver. Another wave removed The Mountain's flank between the

Prow and Russell Cliff. The waves converged downstream and splattered 500 feet up canyon walls as they flowed toward the Puget Lowlands. The Osceola inundated the future townsites of Enumclaw, Buckley, Auburn, Puyallup, Kent, and Tacoma before entering the waters of Puget Sound, 65 miles from The Mountain.

The truncated mountain exploded tephra (ash, pumice and old rocks) from the horseshoe-shaped crater that then occupied its northeast flank. As the Osceola Mudflow defaced the east side, another huge chunk of summit rock between Point Success and Gibraltar Rock rumbled down the south slope of The Mountain forming the Paradise Lahar. The lahar swept 800 feet deep over Paradise Park and spread hydrothermally altered boulders over the meadows. About 2500 years ago, another piece of the old summit crater rim caved off from the wall of Sunset Amphitheater and formed a 1000-foot-high wave (the Round Pass Lahar) that rumbled down the Puyallup Valley.

Lava flows in the east-facing summit depression built up a new summit cone in only 2000 years. Hot tephra and pyroclastic flows repeatedly blanketed the park area, melted ice and snow, and incorporated loose materials in lahars that swamped the Puget Sound basin.

About the year AD 1502, a large piece of clay-rich altered rock broke off from the Sunset Amphitheater. The resulting Electron Mudflow flowed in a wave hundreds of feet deep onto the Puget Lowlands, covering the forested sites of Electron, Orting, and Sumner. Along with occasional landslides, such as the Little Tahoma rockfall avalanche in 1963 and the Russell Cliff rockfall of 1989, glaciers continue to scour, and streams to cut deeper, reducing The Mountain. Hydrothermal alteration continues to weaken The Mountain, though at a very slow rate. Erosion currently outpaces volcanic activity, but the volcanic history of The Mountain shows that when it reawakens, it regrows itself quickly. Fumaroles still keep the summit crater rim free of ice, and small steam and ash eruptions have occurred as recently as 1854. Geologists monitor The Mountain to determine when the injection of new magma will cause its next period of cone building.

ABOVE: Mount Rainier and Spirit Lake seen over the blasted rim of Mount St. Helens. PHOTO ©TYSON FISHER

National Park Service Administration Building, a National Historic Landmark, Longmire District.

PHOTO ©CHARLES GURCHE

RUSTIC ARCHITECTURE

We arrive at the Nisqually Gate of Mount Rainier National Park and know that we enter a special place. Not only is Mount Rainier a refuge of scenic grandeur but also a place where park architecture connects us to the natural scene. Indeed, the massive cedar log gates at Nisqually, Ohanapecosh, White River, and Tipsoo Lake are clear evidence that we have arrived in a cultural landscape where built structures help to shape our sense of place and determine what a national park should look like.

The park's cultural landscape has evolved since 1884, the year the Longmires built a small cabin near the meadow that bears their family name. Since 1903, park road and bridge design has harmonized with superb landscapes and taken advantage of views of mountains, waterfalls, and glaciers. Before the park service was formed in 1916, buildings were utilitarian in design and function and arranged haphazardly. But after that date, the National Park Service organized park development and designed buildings to be attractive and to harmonize with their surroundings.

Park service designers borrowed concepts from rugged Adirondack cabins that used natural wood and "gingerbread" ornamentation. They also took examples of lodges built in the eclectic Swiss Chalet/Alpine Style, then added fine workmanship in wood, metal, and glass from the Craftsman Style. A new style, "Park Service Rustic", emerged in the late 1920s. Mount Rainier became the prototype for the entire National Park System. Architect Tom Vint instituted the park master plan concept at Longmire Village by using a central plaza to unify the space connecting the National Park Inn, the Administration Building, and other public buildings. Designers created a feeling of wilderness by reviving the construction techniques of an earlier era and selecting local glacial boulders and massive timbers to integrate the structures into their natural setting. Characterized by its cedar-shingle gable roof, boulder-faced foundation, log beams, and log-slab siding, the Administration Building, a National Historic Landmark, is a classic example of Park Service Rustic Style.

Today, Mount Rainier National Park remains the most complete example of National Park Service master planning during the 1920s and 1930s. This comprehensive plan made a cohesive unit of the extensive road and trail system, scenic viewpoints, and developed areas that we enjoy today, and laid the foundation for management of 97 percent of the park as wilderness. In 1997, Congress designated the remaining 3 percent of the park as a National Historic Landmark District to protect the integrity of this distinctively American cultural landscape.

OPPOSITE: Stone highway bridge and Christine Falls, Van Trump Creek. PHOTO ©TERRY DONNELLY
PAGE 20/21: Sunrise Day Lodge and Visitor Center, autumn morning. PHOTO ©RON WARFIELD

TOURING THE PARK

Mount Rainier and Kautz Creek.

The Mountain hides from view as I approach via Washington State Route 706 in the Nisqually River Valley. Teasing glimpses of the magnificent ice-covered dome from vantage points in the Cascade foothills sharpen my appetite for a more expansive view. I'm greeted, not by The Mountain, but instead by the forest primeval. The contrast between the human-dominated landscape of managed forests and developments and this quiet green cathedral is like a splash of cold water on the face. As hyper-caffeinated peak-baggers scurry by on their single-goaled quest for "Paradise," I decide to slow down and soak in the sights and sounds of the Old Growth Forest.

It's spring now and lush sword ferns and fiddlehead-stage lady ferns look like the string section of a silent green orchestra. Each day more devils club, bigleaf maple, and vine maple buds expand to fill every open nook in the understory. I watch for oblivious wandering black-tailed deer as the road meanders among the centuries-old trees.

At Kautz Creek, the forest canopy opens and The Mountain pops into view. In 1947, a mudflow surged down this valley and battered the forest with 28-foot-deep mud and debris flows (including automobile-sized boulders). Now, among the snags, a new forest is reclaiming the mudflow deposit in a new cycle of succession.

Spring-fed Longmire Meadow provides the next mountain view. Spring season varies here with the snow line. Sometimes in March, yellow-spathed, giant-leaved skunk cabbage borders the Trail of the Shadows. In years of heavy snow, such as March 1999, the Historic Longmire Walking Tour lies buried under eight feet of snow. I start my tour by visiting "Charlie the Cougar" and his taxidermed friends at the Longmire Museum. The Longmire Museum, built in 1916 as the park's first headquarters, faces the Administration Building near the northern entrance to Longmire Village.

At Christine Falls, a charming stone-faced bridge spans Van Trump Creek along Paradise Road, framing the 40-foot drop from a "hanging" valley. A steep 1.5-mile trail upstream from the nearby trailhead draws me to spectacular 320-foot Comet Falls. In late July, when the snowpack melts, I will ascend another mile to Van Trump Park to enjoy subalpine meadow flowers and Mount Rainier views, often in the company of mountain goats.

The Paradise River plunges over 168-foot Narada Falls about three road miles shy of Paradise. I'll save Paradise for its own visit and turn eastward onto the Stevens Canyon Road toward Ohanapecosh. At dawn or dusk, when The Mountain is visible and the air calm, I marvel at the tranquil beauty of Reflection Lakes. Framed by rising mist, I easily imagine that The Mountain is admiring itself. When breezes chop the reflection, I will clamber up the 1.5-mile steep trail to the Pinnacle Peak saddle for a balcony view of The Mountain.

Autumn comes intensely to the south-facing slopes of Stevens Canyon, where avalanche chutes blaze with the reds, golds, and russet colors of vine maple and mountain ash. From a cirque on Unicorn

OPPOSITE: Western redcedar and vanilla leaf in the old-growth forest of the Nisqually River Valley. PHOTO ©RON WARFIELD

Box Canyon, Muddy Fork of the Cowlitz River.   PHOTO ©FRED HIRSCHMANN

Huckleberry in autumn splendor on Naches Peak.   PHOTO ©CHARLES GURCHE

Peak, Martha Falls drops over a series of ledges, then leaps 125 feet to the floor of the canyon.

At Box Canyon, the broad, glacially carved Cowlitz Valley with its floor of glacial polish and striations contrasts sharply with the narrow gorge of the Cowlitz River. Peering over the edge of the rock-faced bridge, I am impressed by the erosive power of the muddy river churning 180 feet below. Mount Adams, another stratovolcano like Rainier, looms to the south.

Falls Creek appears after I descend road switchbacks into the Ohanapecosh Valley. The popular Grove of the Patriarchs Trail begins nearby and leads to a collection of colossal conifers representative of the old-growth forests that once flourished in the Pacific Northwest lowlands. Touring up the forested corridor northward on Washington State 123, I motor over Cayuse Pass, turn toward Chinook Pass, and notice a puff of steam emanating from Mount St. Helens.

Just west of Chinook Pass—the highest point on the Mather Memorial Parkway, the 75-mile natural corridor over the Cascade Range—I revel in one of the best roadside views in the park. Mount Rainier rises to 14,410 feet in the background, turreted Cowlitz Chimneys and serrated Governors Ridge hold the middle ground, and Tipsoo Lake fills the foreground—often reflecting The Mountain. When flower-lovers crowd the trails of Paradise and Sunrise, rich subalpine meadows on the Natches Peak Loop trail provide enticing floral displays. The flaming colors of autumn fill the meadow in September and early October. Bugling elk break the silence and remind me that seven months of winter will descend upon us soon.

Descending northward on Washington State Route 410, I am rewarded with another magnificent view of Mount Rainier, towering over the old-growth, conifer-covered valley of the White River. The river runs milky with the meltwater from the largest glacier on Mount Rainier, the Emmons. A sharp left turn at the Mather Memorial Parkway monument leads toward Sunrise. As I cross the river, I suddenly recall that when The Mountain collapsed 5600 years ago, the Osceola Mudflow was more than 500 feet thick at this location. Parking the car, I start out walking, scurrying upward from the peaceful old-growth forest of western hemlock, western redcedar, and Douglas-fir, through a noble fir zone, to top out at Sunrise Ridge in a sparse canopy of subalpine fir, Alaska yellow-cedar, and whitebark pine. Automobile travelers observe that Mount Rainier looms even larger from Sunrise Point, but The Mountain seems almost benign now, its volcanic heat cloaked by the Emmons and Winthrop glaciers.

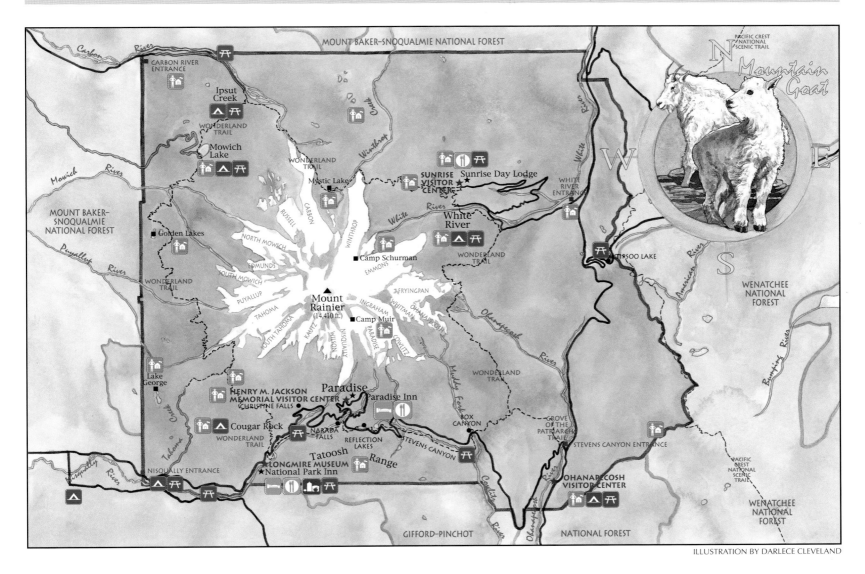

ILLUSTRATION BY DARLECE CLEVELAND

Established on March 2, 1899, Mount Rainier National Park protects a 235,625-acre arctic-alpine masterpiece, its emerald setting of old-growth coniferous forest, and the richest subalpine meadows on the planet.

The active volcano, draped by 25 named glaciers, lies west of the Cascade Crest moisture barrier, so it becomes a prime target for a procession of eastward-flowing Pacific storms. Lower slopes, often enveloped in clouds and fog, receive prodigious amounts of rain; higher slopes garner world-record snowfalls. Visitors seeking flower-filled subalpine meadows arrive in late July or early August. Skiers and snowshoers find snow cover from November through May or June.

Ninety-seven percent of the park is designated wilderness, where hikers can find solitude or encounter a cougar, elk, or mountain goat on 240 miles of maintained trail. The 90-mile Wonderland Trail circles The Mountain and provides access to forest, meadows, and glaciers.

Most visitors arrive via State Route 706 and enter the park at the Nisqually Entrance on a beeline to Paradise. At Longmire Village, the National Park Inn offers food, lodging, and gifts. The Longmire Museum provides information on natural and cultural history in displays from an earlier era. The Wilderness Information Center in the Administration Building issues backcountry permits in summer only.

At the first heavy snowfall of winter, the road beyond Longmire is gated at night, reopening daily to Paradise when plowed. Stevens Canyon Road and State Routes 410 and 123 remain closed in winter from the first heavy snowfall in November, reopening in May or June when plowing is completed. The Sunrise Road closes in early October and reopens by July 1.

At Paradise, the historic Paradise Inn offers food, lodging, and gifts (mid-May through early October). Climbers receive permits at the Guide House in summer and at the Henry M. Jackson Memorial Visitor Center (summer and winter weekends).

Ohanapecosh Visitor Center in the southeast corner of the park offers exhibits on old-growth forest ecology and human history, in summer only.

At Sunrise in the northeast part of the park, at elevation 6400 feet, the Day Lodge offers food and gifts but no lodging. The Sunrise Visitor Center provides information, exhibits, and book sales.

Front-country automobile campgrounds are located at Ipsut Creek (check road conditions before visiting), Sunshine Point (open year round), Cougar Rock (open late May to early October), Ohanapecosh (late May through early October), and White River (mid-June through mid-September).

MOUNT RAINIER
THE CENTERPIECE

Sunrise silhouette of Mount Rainier.   PHOTO ©KIRKENDALL–SPRING

Of all the fire mountains which, like beacons,
once blazed along the Pacific Coast,
Mount Rainier is the noblest in form.   —John Muir

To everyone who sees it, Mount Rainier is THE Mountain. Its 14,410-foot dome projects majestically 7000 to 9000 feet above all its neighbors. The Mountain reposes in ice-covered silence, belying the fact that it is the most dangerous volcano in America. Mount Rainier is the highest peak in the Cascade Range, a chain of volcanoes that extends from British Columbia to northern California. The Cascades compose the Pacific Northwest section of the "Ring of Fire," a zone of active volcanoes and frequent earthquakes that rims the Pacific Ocean.

Though its craggy shape gives the impression of great age, Mount Rainier is a young stratovolcano whose slopes are rapidly changing. The Mountain shows the results of the dramatic interplay of volcanic mountain building and the erosive agents of ice and gravity. In human context, The Mountain seldom erupts, but geologically recent eruptions and collapse events have been more destructive than the familiar events occurring at neighboring Mount St. Helens.

Viewed from the west, at Gobblers Knob, the classic cone shape is truncated into three separate peaks: Liberty Cap, Columbia Crest, and Point Success. The broad Puyallup Glacier occupies a cirque beneath Sunset Amphitheater, a huge bow-shaped scar left by the Round Pass and Electron debris flows.

From the south, at Paradise, The Mountain appears as a broad dome with Point Success and Gibraltar Rock contrasting with snowfields and the Nisqually Glacier. From the east, at Sunrise, Emmons and Winthrop glaciers shroud lava flows that have partially filled the horseshoe-shaped Osceola collapse basin. But Little Tahoma and Steamboat Prow remain after glaciers and other erosional forces have removed most of Mount Rainier's original surface. From the north, Carbon Glacier has incised older lava flows to form the largest cirque in the Cascade Range.

An active volcano is overwhelmingly beautiful, but demands respect and vigilance to avoid being caught unprepared by one of its geologic tantrums. Though geologists do not expect future lava flows or pyroclastic flows to exit the park, their eruptive products will certainly melt some of the 34 square miles of permanent snow and ice covering The Mountain. As they have often in the past, the resulting floods and lahars will sweep like churning masses of wet concrete down valleys radiating from the volcano to inundate urban developments as far away as Tacoma and Auburn.

Intense rainfall and glacial outburst floods will frequently cause slurries of mud and truck-sized boulders to inundate valley bottoms within the park. Rockfall avalanches, like the Little Tahoma Rockfall of 1963 that splattered millions of tons of rock onto Emmons Glacier, will continue to reduce the mass of The Mountain. Hydrothermal alteration continues to weaken the rock, making it susceptible to another

OPPOSITE: Clearing fog and tarn in Moraine Park. PHOTO ©ALAN MAJCHROWICZ   **PAGE 28/29:** Mount Rainier seen from Reflection Lakes. PHOTO ©LARRY CARVER

Lenticular cloud above The Mountain   PHOTO ©RON WARFIELD

Mount Rainier and Tipsoo Lake reflections, dawn.   PHOTO ©TERRY DONNELLY

large debris flow event similar to the 500-year-old Electron mud-flow that inundated the Puget Sound lowlands. It's only slightly reassuring that these big sector collapse events occur infrequently (on average, every 500 to 1000 years) because landslide triggers, such as earthquakes, can occur without warning.

Rainier stands directly in the path of wet air masses streaming eastward from the Pacific. Successive winter storms pound The Mountain from October through May, with only brief intermittent sunbreaks. Fog, rain, or even snow showers can shroud The Mountain's slopes in summer.

The 14,410-foot mountain rises so far above the surrounding landscape that it appears to make its own weather. Wind flowing over The Mountain forms a standing wave pattern in the air. Moisture of an approaching storm enters the wave and condenses into a lenticular cloud as it rises and cools in passing over The Mountain. The cloud stays in place as it continually forms on the windward ascending side of the wave and evaporates on the descending leeward side.

When the clouds part, I stop in my tracks and gaze in wonderment. The Mountain, in all its snow-covered majesty, looms huge and dazzlingly beautiful. Like a little kid, I easily get excited describing my favorite locations to view Mount Rainier, lapsing into hyperbole in the face of a place that defies words. Standing on the crest of the Tatoosh Range, after a short but steep trail to Pinnacle Peak saddle, I catch first light on the grand stage of forest, meadow, glaciers, and The Mountain. This and the roadside scene from Tipsoo Lake provide balcony views. With a little more effort, I gain a front row seat and experience Mount Rainier's geology directly in front of me. At Emerald Ridge, I touch the noisy snout of the Tahoma Glacier and feel its erosive power. At Third Burroughs Mountain, I face massive ice and the scene of one of the world's greatest landslides, the Osceola. I come to this place of quiet refuge to contemplate my own insignificance. Even though I have stood on Rainier's summit and enjoyed the most sublime view of sunrise over a sea of clouds, I agree with John Muir when he wrote "more pleasure is to be found at the foot of mountains than on their frozen tops." Find your own personal place on Mount Rainier, absorb its supernatural power, and then protect it for your children.

Climber silhouetted at Camp Muir with Mount Adams in distance.

CLIMBING MOUNT RAINIER

The Mountain's icy crown, at 14,410 feet the fifth highest in the contiguous United States, invites climbers from around the world to test their skills against its rigors. Mountaineers rate routes on The Mountain's north side, such as Curtis and Liberty ridges, among the classic alpine climbs on the planet. The sight of house-sized ice chunks plummeting a vertical mile during an avalanche daunts even experienced climbers, who are used to braving conditions like those on the world's highest summits. Of the 11,000 climbers who annually make the attempt, only half gain the summit in this most sublime Cascades excursion.

Rainier's first passionate climbing enthusiast was Lieutenant August V. Kautz, who reached the saddle between Point Success and Columbia Crest in 1857. Several other climbing parties may have summited The Mountain in the 1850s. The first climbers to fully document a successful climb arrived in 1870. Assisted by James Longmire and led partway by the Indian Sluiskin, Hazard Stevens and Philemon B. Van Trump waved a flag on the summit on August 17, 1870. Van Trump returned in 1883 with Longmire and George Bayley, and again in 1888 to accompany naturalist John Muir. Muir's lyric account of the trip stirred enthusiastic climbers and scientists to help establish Mount Rainier National Park in 1899. In 1890, Fay Fuller, a young schoolteacher from Yelm, Washington, donned boys' boots and heavy flannels, grasped her homemade alpenstock, and became the first woman to summit The Mountain.

Fay returned in 1897, with 200 members of Portland's Mazama Club and summited with 57 others: mass pleasure seeking had replaced solitude. Professor Edgar McClure carried a mercury barometer to the summit, then fell on his moonlight return. He was Rainier's first climbing fatality.

Throughout the 1920s, outdoor clubs climbed in large groups. Stephen Mather, who became the first director of the National Park Service in 1916, climbed with the Sierra Club in 1905. During the 1940s, 50s, and 60s, an outbreak of "Mountain fever" led to many high routes being pioneered on The Mountain. Local brothers Lou and Jim Whittaker guided and trained on Rainier, and Jim became the first American to summit Everest in 1963.

Mount Rainier now attracts a new generation of speed climbers, snowboarders, winter climbers, and ski mountaineers. Their high-tech gear, easy road access, modern climbing techniques, current weather forecasts, and professional guide services make the summit accessible.

31

PARADISE
THE SOUTH SIDE

Paradise Inn: a National Historic Landmark.   PHOTO ©RON WARFIELD

My heart takes a joyful leap. I'm standing in the midst of the most luxuriant subalpine floral displays on planet Earth. Martha Longmire visited in 1885 and exclaimed, "It looks just like Paradise." Since then Paradise has been the focus of millions of flower lovers and the most popular starting point for climbers of The Mountain.

Today, I arrive before sunrise to begin a search for the visual essence of Paradise. It's late July and a carpet of fragrant blue lupine has finally replaced snowbanks that were ringed by white avalanche lilies and golden glacier lilies only two weeks ago. A black-tailed deer springs away as I ascend the Dead Horse Creek Trail. The balsam scent of subalpine fir fills my nose as a pair of gray jays swoops overhead on their way to greet the dawn.

Beyond the Paradise weather station, where 1122 inches of snow fell in 1971-72, the Nisqually Glacier grinds from the summit toward Nisqually Vista. A rumbling avalanche on the glacier breaks the silence as sun strikes the upper mountain. I hurry past masses of lupine, magenta paintbrush, Sitka valerian, and bistort for a better view. I notice that orange and brown boulders lie scattered among the floral displays. All is quiet now, but these hydrothermally altered rocks remind me that the Paradise Lahar dropped these lava specimens from Rainier's summit when the 800-foot deep wave thundered over Paradise Valley only 5600 years ago. In a trailside cut, I find a multilayered column of gritty pumice. The luxuriant wildflowers that carpet the meadow grow upon the fertile remains of countless explosive eruptions from Mounts Rainier, St. Helens, and Mazama. I'm walking on the shoulder of an ACTIVE volcano.

Near Glacier Vista, The Mountain and the glacier overwhelm my flower-filled viewfinder. I share my viewpoint with a hoary marmot sampling its way through the floral profusion. Near Pebble Creek, I spy a ptarmigan nipping buds from a mat of pink mountain heather. These plants have survived the snows and winds of seven thousand winters, but they are no match for hikers' boots, which easily destroy their fragile roots.

Beyond the tree limit, at 6900-foot Panorama Point, views over the jagged summits of the Tatoosh Range open up to include other Cascade stratovolcanoes to the south—Mounts Adams, Hood, and St. Helens. Behind me, mountaineers stomp up the Muir Snowfield on their way to Mount Rainier's summit.

In the valley 1400 feet below lies Paradise Inn and Henry M. Jackson Memorial Visitor Center, dots of human development in the distance. Opened in 1917, the inn is a National Historic Landmark building recognized for its contribution to rustic architecture in the National Park System and its importance in creating an American sense of place.

Descending the Skyline Trail, I enjoy white saxifrage and pink monkey flower growing along meltwater streamlets that coalesce and splash over Sluiskin Falls. Midday fog envelops me as I clamber over glacial polish and striations left when the Paradise Glacier melted into oblivion.

OPPOSITE: Lifting morning fog in the wildflower meadows of Paradise. PHOTO ©TERRY DONNELLY

Myrtle Falls, Edith Creek Basin above Paradise.
PHOTO ©RON WARFIELD

The fog dissipates as I hike through Edith Creek Basin. The Mountain catches afternoon sidelight behind silhouetted subalpine fir and mountain hemlock above AltaVista. Near Myrtle Falls, as I marvel at the mop-head appearance of western anemone seedheads, I hear the distress whistle of a hoary marmot and notice a Cascade red fox carrying a meadow vole. Like me, the marmot will get to enjoy another day in Paradise.

Returning in mid-winter, I find a monochrome white world, buried under a 20-foot-deep snowpack. The "average" winter drops as much as 680 inches of snowfall on Paradise. On winter weekends, when The Mountain is "out," Paradise becomes Puget Sound Municipal Park for cross-country skiers, snowboarders, and snow players. To avoid the crowds, I come on Wednesday, bringing snowshoes, so that I can enjoy the egret-plumed hemlocks by myself. In the 1940s, a thousand US Army ski troopers trained at Paradise, then a nationally recognized ski area. The soldiers climbed to Rainier's summit to test clothing and skied 90 miles around The Mountain carrying rifles and 85-pound packs.

Today, I stuff lunch and a camera in a daypack and head for Mazama Ridge. A pair of ravens chortles in the snow-covered treetops as gray jays follow my progress. I trace the tracks of a snowshoe hare, and later a ptarmigan, but see neither—their white camouflage is working. Pine martens and red foxes had followed the same paths earlier, with different interest. The snowpack insulates pikas and meadow voles that remain active at the ground surface.

I top out on Mazama Ridge only 1.5 raven miles from the Paradise parking lot. It is a scene of winter solitude. Spirelike subalpine firs and droopy-topped mountain hemlocks, festooned by three weeks of snowfall, cast polar bear shadows on the frozen scene. A small lenticular cloud caps The Mountain, alerting me that the next winter storm will soon break this perfect stillness. Twenty feet beneath my snowshoes the hoary marmot hibernates for eight months, saving energy for next summer's glorious rush. But, the avalanche lilies do not wait. Their bulb tips grow in anticipation of summer and will melt their way upward through the thinning snow next June, when winter loses its grip. I troop back toward civilization as low-angle late afternoon light casts a warm silvery glow on the crystalline scene. In the hour before sunset, I grasp the meaning of Paradise.

Mount Rainier, winter at Paradise.
PHOTO ©GREG PROBST

Profuse wildflower display on Mazama Ridge.

PHOTO ©TERRY DONNELLY

SUBALPINE WILDFLOWERS

Between the lowland forests and the perpetual snow and ice on the upper mountain lies a zone of the loveliest flowers, so luxuriant that naturalist John Muir declared the flower-filled meadows of Paradise to be the richest subalpine garden he had ever found. Emerging from 20-foot-deep winter snowpacks, usually by mid-July, a profusion of flowers spreads over Paradise and other meadows known locally as "parks." Scattered in a zone between 5000 to 8000 feet in elevation, the floral parks encircle The Mountain.

Winter storms bring more moisture to Rainier's western and southwestern parks, places such as Indian Henry's Hunting Ground, Van Trump Park, Sunset Park, and Spray Park. Small rivulets harbor pink monkey flower, shooting star, and willow herb. Yellow glacier lily, white avalanche lily, and cream-colored western anemone carpet every available slope around receding snowbanks. Successive waves of floral color wash over the meadow each week as summer progresses. Subalpine lupine forms a fragrant blue carpet, accented by magenta paintbrush, and white Sitka valerian and bistort. Later, arnica and senecio add yellow among masses of lavender fleabane and aster. Purple gentian and pearly everlasting close out the season.

The rain-shadow effect of The Mountain, together with well-drained pumice soils on eastern-side parks such as Summerland, Grand Park, and Yakima Park (Sunrise), favors drought-tolerant species such as groundsel, buckwheat, wallflower, sedge and grass, which thrive alongside lily, lupine, and aster.

Near the upper limit of the meadows, alpine fellfields (rock lands) and heath communities comprise a band of specialized perennial plants that grow low to the ground in cushions, rosettes, or mats to cope with nightly freezing conditions, drying winds, and abrasion by wind-blown ice, snow, and pebbles. These tiny plants bloom lavishly out of proportion to their stature and tough habitat. Stones hold loose pumice soils in place and protect the plants from wind and needle ice, which uproot the plants.

Alpine heath communities of pink and white heather have been growing continuously for more than 7000 years, qualifying them among earth's oldest living things. Ironically, these fragile heather and fellfield communities are located in areas that are favored by hikers and mountaineers. Plants that have survived centuries of ashfall, eruption, avalanche, and ice storm will require our respect and patience to prevent further trampling and erosion.

PAGE 36/37: Mount Rainier towers above a profuse wildflower display on Mazama Ridge. PHOTO ©TERRY DONNELLY

Sunrise
The East Side

White River and Mount Rainier.

PHOTO ©FRED HIRSCHMANN

Fog lies thick as I begin my climb out of the old-growth forest of the White River Valley. I'm looking for dawn's first light on Mount Rainier in a place called Sunrise. My enthusiasm is rewarded as I round the hairpin turn at Sunrise Point. The Mountain glows in the moonlight as it projects above the sea of clouds that laps at the base of Cowlitz Chimneys. The Chimneys are the jagged remains of volcanoes that preceded Mount Rainier by tens of millions of years. Farther to the south, two stratovolcanos—Mount Adams and Mount Hood—penetrate the silvery cloud layer. On the ice-covered face of Mount Rainier, I spy a row of tiny lights—the headlamps of summit-seeking mountaineers who have been climbing for hours on the Emmons Glacier.

As the faint magenta glow on The Mountain brightens into yellows and oranges, the stars and moon fade into a turquoise sky. Moments later, the sun strikes the summit in a pink glow. For an instant, the massive ice-covered dome seems awash in a blaze of color. Then, in the time it takes me to don some mittens and sip a cup of tea, The Mountain transforms into dazzling white.

I arrive at Sunrise about the same time as those climbers reach the summit. The subalpine meadow at this 6400-foot elevation looks different from the vegetation of Paradise. The rain shadow of Mount Rainier allows much less precipitation to fall here than on the southwestern side of The Mountain. The soil is much more porous because walnut-sized pumice fragments from Rainier's numerous post-glacial explosive eruptions litter the surface. Glacier and avalanche lily, lupine, and aster bloom here in abundance but grasses and sedges are more conspicuous than at Paradise. Sunrise lies just above the upper limit of continuous forest. Subalpine fir grows in atolls scattered about the meadows. Mountain hemlock, familiar at Paradise, is nearly absent, replaced by clumps of whitebark pine. A few contorted Alaska yellow-cedars cling to Sourdough Ridge.

Park service master planning in 1928 called for development of three hotels to take visitor pressures off Paradise—one each at Spray Park, Sunset Park, and Yakima Park—all to be connected by new roads around The Mountain. Instead, only one was built, at Yakima Park (Sunrise). The other areas became part of undeveloped wilderness, beyond the reach of automobiles. Opened in 1931, the Sunrise development was conceived to be a fully planned cohesive unit aesthetically and historically connected to the scenic grandeur. The park service chose a "frontier" theme based on Northwest fur trading defensive structures and decided on blockhouses to fit this cultural setting. The new developments were named Sunrise. Eighty years earlier, Owhi, a chief of the Yakama tribe, had hunted, harvested, danced, and played games in this summering ground called *Me-yah-ah Pah*, "the place of the chief."

The park service constructed a log blockhouse in 1931 and added a second blockhouse and a community house in 1943. The community house later became the Sunrise Visitor Center when interpretive exhibits were added. Only a single wing of the original proposed hotel was built. It still serves as the day lodge without guest rooms—a shingle-covered monument to its unfulfilled potential.

I find Emmons Vista Nature Trail across from the lodge and walk 800 feet to an eye-popping view. Emmons Glacier flows 9000 feet from Rainier's ice-covered dome to terminate in the White River Valley. Purple-

OPPOSITE: Breaking storm at dawn seen from Yakima Park, near Sunrise. PHOTO ©FRED HIRSCHMANN

Early-morning light from near Sunrise.

gray jumbled rocks masking the glacier's snout fell from jagged Little Tahoma peak in 1963. Fire-killed trees along Sunrise Rim in the Silver Forest provide a picturesque foreground to frame this kaleidoscope of glaciers, lahars, and rock falls.

Climbing gradually on the Sourdough Ridge Trail, I'm joined by a group of elk, some of the 800 to 1200 animals that graze in the park's eastside meadows. As the elk cross the ridge and descend into Huckleberry Park, I hike eastward along the ridge to Dege Peak to take in the classic Cascade view of Mount Rainier towering above a panorama of summits.

I remain on the ridge and climb westward toward Burroughs Mountain. On the talus slope near Frozen Lake, I hear a familiar "eenk" and stop to watch a colony of pikas prepare for next winter's feast.

A band of mountain goats ranges on the slopes of Mount Fremont. Unlike the introduced goats at Olympic National Park, these goats are native and well adapted to life in Rainier's arctic-alpine environment. Their white coats give them the look of tiny snow patches on the tundra.

Beyond Frozen Lake, I scramble over a steep snowbank and enter the treeless tundra zone on First Burroughs Mountain. At first, it looks like a rock-covered desert but closer inspection reveals mats and cushions of tiny plants hugging the ground between wind-blocking rocks of the fellfields. Scarlet cliff paintbrush, alpine golden daisy, and alpine lupine dazzle with color among pincushions of moss campion and spreading phlox. Humbled by the tenacity of tundra plants, I tread softly in this land of floral wonders; it belongs to our grandchildren, and to the marmots.

Standing on the top of Third Burroughs, I stare up nearly 6500 feet to the top of Mount Rainier and peer straight down onto the crevasse-riddled Winthrop Glacier. This is where I feel closest to The Mountain.

The Emmons Glacier.

GLACIERS

Mount Rainier lies in the wake of wet Pacific storms that dump an annual average 680 inches of snow on Paradise. Some snow remains on the upper mountain at the end of the summer melt season and compacts into the summit ice cap and 25 glaciers radiating from The Mountain. Nearly 34 square miles of ice envelops The Mountain—the largest single-peak glacial system in the contiguous United States. This cubic mile of ice exceeds the volume on all other Cascade volcanoes combined.

Several times in the last 75,000 years glaciers covered The Mountain and extended all the way to the Puget Lowlands. These glaciers carved cirques on The Mountain's flanks, scoured valleys, undercut ridges, and deposited debris throughout the park. Early glaciers removed nearly one third of the volume of Mount Rainier, but the glaciers that survive on The Mountain today date only from the Little Ice Age that climaxed before 1840.

Glaciers reflect changes in climate; if snowfall exceeds melt, the terminus advances; extra melt causes recession. Nisqually Glacier, easily observed from Nisqually and Glacier vistas at Paradise, exhibits classic alpine glacial features. Crevasses in the icefall on the upper glacier and the chocolate color of meltwater at its terminus attest that the Nisqually still actively carves The Mountain. Climax moraines of the 1840s record the terminus retreat upvalley of more than a mile. The glacier has been thinning and retreating since the late 1980s.

Nisqually, Kautz, South Tahoma, and Winthrop Glaciers have been the source of *jokulhlaups*, glacial outburst floods, in recent decades. These outbursts deposit masses of water, mud, ice chunks, and boulders in debris flows far downvalley, damaging roads and structures.

Cowlitz-Ingraham Glacier once extended 65 miles downvalley, the farthest of any Rainier ice-age glacier. It now is thinning and retreating rapidly. An artifact of global warming, the deglacierized site of Paradise Glacier now lies strewn with boulders atop polished and striated bedrock.

Emmons Glacier, with a surface area of more than four square miles, the largest glacier by area in the contiguous United States, drapes over lava flows from the summit cone and obscures the Osceola collapse crater.

Sheltered by Rainier, Carbon Glacier, the thickest (700 feet), most voluminous (.2 cubic miles), and longest (5.7 miles) glacier on The Mountain extends to a lower elevation (3500 feet) than any other glacier in the contiguous United States.

OHANAPECOSH
THE SOUTHEAST SIDE

Western redcedar and decomposing western hemlock, Grove of The Patriarchs.   PHOTO ©TERRY DONNELLY

Standing on the lip of a rock, I gaze at thundering Silver Falls on the Ohanapecosh River. The river pours through a narrow slot canyon in volcanic rocks 40 million years older than Mount Rainier—the Ohanapecosh Formation. I come here twice a year. In April or May, when 20-foot-deep snowpacks still bury the subalpine meadows of Paradise and Sunrise, and spring showers douse the valleys on the park's western side, I come to this slightly drier side to absorb the green wonders of the season. Melting snow pours extra volume into the river, so the rock I'm standing on shakes at the equivalent of 3.8 on the Richter scale. Mist from the 40-foot falls freshens mosses and lichens in the gorge downstream, maintaining a velvet emerald surface on the canyon walls. Unlike other glacial streams in the park, the Ohanapecosh River runs a luminescent turquoise color, an effect caused by the scattering of light by colloidal-sized rock particles suspended in the water. Giant peeled logs piled up at the base of the falls attest to the fact that floods sometimes scour vegetation from this valley, resetting the forest succession clock. I like to arrive when dogwood blooms along the river. At this time, I look more closely to find delicate calypso orchid and trillium growing in the shade of the old-growth canopy.

When the first heavy rains of September and October strike the upper slopes of The Mountain and mantle the meadows with snow, I return to Ohanapecosh to find autumn in full glory. The dark green shades of western hemlock and Douglas-fir contrast sharply with small splashes and bands of vibrant golds, rusts, and crimson on the forest floor. Pacific dogwood flashes red and yellow as vine maple blazes with the colors of fire. The soaring pillars of tree trunks seem taller when framed by yellow bigleaf maple and tiny huckleberry leaves. Elk and black-tailed deer migrate to the lower forest zone in autumn to add the colorful vegetation to their winter diet. Douglas squirrels chatter in the treetops while they gather cones and seeds for winter.

A few miles downstream from Silver Falls is another rock where generations of Taidnapam tribal fishermen have stood for 3600 years to dip-net fish. Their word for standing on the lip of a rock is Ohanapecosh. Taidnapams and other Indian people visited Ohanapecosh Hot Springs long before they were discovered by pioneers in 1906. Along with Longmire, these springs became the place to "take the waters." In 1925, a small log-and-cedar shake rustic lodge, 31 cabins, and a bathhouse offered mineral baths. The concession was removed in the 1960s and the springs allowed to revert to a natural state. Now, in winter, only elk wallow in the warm spring water. In summer, the Ohanapecosh Campground offers a cooler "wet west side" forest setting to visitors escaping the heat of central Washington.

My first learning experience with old-growth forest came decades ago when a park ranger at the original Forest House Museum helped me discover the big old trees at Ohanapecosh. A modern visitor center now carries the forest theme to new generations of tree lovers.

About one half-mile upriver from Silver Falls, I traverse an old avalanche chute covered by red alder and vine maple. In this forest of giant conifers, alders are among the first colonizers when storms,

---

OPPOSITE: Western redcedar and hemlock above the Ohanapecosh River. PHOTO ©LARRY ULRICH   **PAGE 44/45:** Silver Falls on the Ohanapecosh River. PHOTO ©RON WARFIELD

Falls Creek Falls.

floods, avalanches, or fires create an opening. Alders have nodules on their roots that fix nitrogen from the air, building new soil. In closed-canopy forests, nitrogen fixing is done by lichens growing in the crowns of mature conifers.

After walking along the valley margin, I notice my forest friends—rough-barked Douglas-fir, straight-boled western hemlock, and buttress-based western redcedar—suddenly take on the aura of great age. Some leaning cedars and fallen firs show the effects of fires that have raced through the valley several times in the last millennium.

A light drizzle freshens the lichens growing on cedars leaning over the river. It's quiet except for the patter of fog-drip on the gently flowing river. A pair of varied thrushes announces their presence, sounding like steam whistles. As I step across a bridge onto an island terrace in the river, I get the feeling of entering a cathedral — not one of stone and glass, but of trees. A winter wren sings welcome as I pass a diverging pair of upturned rootwads. In the presence of big old trees that have avoided fire for ten centuries, I am joyful that I can share a moment in the time continuum that sustains us both.

These 900-year-old trees have survived the assault of storms and floods since the time when the Normans conquered England. However, trees in the Grove of the Patriarchs already show signs of an overdose of wonder and awe. Bark on the largest tree in the Grove, an 11-foot diameter western redcedar, has been rubbed smooth by the adoring hands of countless visitors. Its knobby-buttressed roots lie exposed by the bootsteps of seekers of longevity. Perhaps we could tread more lightly so that the base of these timeless trees could once more be carpeted by oxalis, vanilla leaf, and oak fern. Then these giants might continue to teach us that board feet are not the only measure of the old-growth forest.

Ancient western redcedars in Grove of The Patriarchs.

Old-growth forest above the Ohanapecosh River.

OLD GROWTH FORESTS

When Congress established Mount Rainier National Park in 1899, an unbroken expanse of old-growth forest extended from The Mountain all the way to the shores of Puget Sound. Since then, except in protected wilderness or national parks like Mount Rainier, clearcutting has felled the old forests. The green stillness of the remaining forest greets us with timeless serenity.

Plentiful rainfall and moderate temperatures provide ideal conditions for the growth of the world's greatest stand of conifers. Douglas-fir six feet in diameter, ancient Sitka spruce, western hemlock, and western redcedar with 11-foot girths command attention and confirm that this ecosystem has been developing for hundreds of years.

Big old trees, a diversity of age and species, standing snags, an open, spacious, multilayered canopy, large downed logs, logs in streams, and lush groundcover define the old-growth forests. It takes at least 250 to 300 years after disturbance to develop this character.

In these dense forests, nitrogen is in short supply. But many of the lichens that grow on the upper limbs and bark of mature trees contain cyanobacteria that fix nitrogen from the air. Rain and wind carry the nitrogen to the soil surface. Mycorrhizal fungi absorb soil nitrogen and transfer water and nutrients to myriad tree roots that support the forest canopy.

Northern flying squirrels live quietly in the treetops and drop nightly to the forest floor to eat truffles—the fruiting bodies of fungi. The squirrels spread fungal spores wrapped in packets of fertilizer and become food for saw-whet and northern spotted owls. Storms, fire, and disease batter the treetops creating snags and bring an occasional giant crashing to the forest floor. Snags provide nesting sites for owls, swifts, woodpeckers, and bats. Downed logs become habitat for small mammals, reptiles, amphibians, a host of invertebrates, nitrogen-fixing bacteria, and truffle-producing fungi. A new generation of trees takes root in these "nurse logs" and adds biomass as the centuries pass.

The rhythm of recycling in the old-growth forest involves a multitude of wonders, from giant trees to tiny microbes, working in harmony with an economy of energy and resources. The processes that support these awesome trees also maintain us. Standing close to these forest giants inspires hope that we can live in peace with our world.

CARBON RIVER/ MOWICH LAKE

THE NORTHWEST SIDE

Avalanche lilies in fog near Mowich Lake.   PHOTO ©KIRKENDALL–SPRING

It's raining so hard that even the banana slugs are taking cover. This first storm of the winter season reminds me that I'm in the rain forest of the Carbon River Valley where more than 80 inches of rain fall each year. The river normally runs a milky color over a broad boulder-choked, u-shaped valley bottom—Carbon Glacier is just upstream. Today this usually gentle-flowing, narrow-channeled braided stream is angrily rearranging the boulders in its bed and carrying huge logs in its chocolate-colored flow. I'm witnessing a flash flood that might reset the successional clock of the old-growth forest. Some of these trees have avoided floods for 10 centuries.

A Douglas-fir more than nine feet in diameter is inconspicuous among its peers in this land of giant trees. Western hemlock and western redcedar vie for size records as well. The presence of Sitka spruce signals that I'm walking in a temperate rain forest even though we are more than 100 miles inland from the ocean. This is a world apart. Dense shade and filtered light reaching the forest floor support a lush undergrowth of sword ferns, vine maple, skunk cabbage, and devils club. Lichens and mosses festoon every branch in the canopy, while mosses and ferns carpet every downed log and boulder. Overhead, rare marbled murrelets burrow into luxuriant pillows of moss to make their nests. The murrelets fly fifty miles to Puget Sound to feed.

The five-mile-long road from the Carbon River Entrance to Ipsut Creek winds unpaved through the forest. Storms in the last decade have changed the river's course, damaged the roadway at Falls Creek, and piled 500-year-old trees into logjams. When the road is closed by floods, it becomes a quiet old-growth portal. When open, the road offers access to Ranger, Chenuis, and Ipsut waterfalls, reached via short trails through groves of giant trees.

Three miles upriver from the Ipsut Creek trailhead, I cross a sturdy but easily swayed suspension bridge across the Carbon River. In the early 1920s, the National Park Service built a road to Cataract Creek near this point. Thankfully, plans to connect this road with the White River and Westside roads in a grand "Around-the-Mountain" road never materialized. Now, when crowds inundate Paradise, I take refuge in this quiet corner of the park.

My nerves are steadied by the magnificent view upstream. The rock-covered snout of Carbon Glacier extends to 3500 feet in a narrow gorge just upvalley. Behind it, Mount Rainier rises to 14,410 feet in ice-covered majesty only 6.5 miles away. Avalanches seem to float down the 3600-foot cliff of Willis Wall, the face of the biggest cirque in the Cascades. Liberty Ridge, one of the planet's classic climbs, juts directly toward the summit. The glacier's snout has retreated slightly since its minor advance of the 1970s, when it crushed vegetation with boulders rolling off its terminus. I watch the snout from a respectful distance as the debris-covered glacier snout spits rocks onto the moraine forming at its base. The blue ice carries a heavy load of rock—the product of the glacier's plucking, and of numerous debris falls.

On a better day, beargrass blooms on the shore of Eunice Lake as I arrive after a three-mile hike

OPPOSITE: Beargrass below Mount Rainier, Spray Park. PHOTO ©MARY LIZ AUSTIN

Spray Falls.

Old growth in the Carbon River Rain Forest.

from Mowich Lake. Subalpine fir frames the glacier-clad dome of Mount Rainier reflected in the deep blue water. I decide to ascend the ridge for a better view. Tolmie Peak, with its historically intact fire lookout, offers a vast panoramic view, with Mount Baker and Glacier Peak in the north, the Olympics in the west, and Mount St. Helens in the south. To the southeast, Mount Rainier looms over the sparkling waters of Eunice and Mowich lakes. Dr. William Fraser Tolmie did not climb this peak named for him when he came to collect herbs in 1833. Instead, he probably climbed Hessong Rock, closer to The Mountain. I would be happy to bask in this view until sunset but fog has crept in to bathe the scene in moist gray softness. On the return to Mowich, I admire the work of park staff and volunteers in restoring the subalpine meadows after campers and meadow stompers had trampled the fragile vegetation.

Every Mount Rainier hiking connoisseur has their favorite subalpine meadow: mine may be the scenery-packed Spray Park. Fan-shaped Spray Falls splashes 350 feet over a double-tiered rock face, a stunning sight near the meadow. In the 1920s, park concessionaires envisioned building a grand hotel at Spray Park, as an alternative to crowded Paradise. The hotel and access road were never built, but thousands of campers and day hikers arrived and severely impacted these meadows. Since the 1970s, camping has been prohibited to allow recovery of the floral profusion. Now, in late July when avalanche lilies fill every nook and cranny, Spray Park becomes the supreme wildflower meadow in the park. Glacier lily and buttercup rim every receding snowbank. Groves of subalpine fir and mountain hemlock, interspersed with heather meadows, frame every view. Glacial tarns scattered about the meadows delight photographers and display superb evening reflections of the Mountain. Fellfields and heather meadows draw me to the 6400-foot ridgeline for an ethereal view down into flower-filled Mist Park and Seattle Park. I walk back through masses of waist-deep subalpine lupine as sunset flames The Mountain. It's a four-mile hike by moonlight back to camp at Mowich Lake.

Mount Rainier seen from Klapatche Park, sunset.

Just as the summit trip challenges climbers, so, too, the 90-mile Wonderland Trail, which encircles Mount Rainier, lays down the gauntlet for hikers. This is the experience of a lifetime. The total elevation gain (and loss) on the loop is about 20,000 feet—more than that of a summit climb. There is satisfaction in the feat itself, but the essence of the trail is in its name: **Wonder**. The wonder of the Wonderland lies in the trail's passage through every life zone of the park, winding from lower old-growth forests to flower-filled subalpine meadows, beside glacial streams and tarns, and across barren rock and snow. The trail reaches the snouts of three major glaciers—Tahoma, Carbon, and Winthrop—and provides views of all 25 glaciers on The Mountain. Along the way, the trail climbs and descends steeply, giving magnificent views that change continually in angle and mood.

The Wonderland Trail follows a roughly similar route to the one blazed in 1915 by a 102-member party of The Mountaineers, which made the first expedition around The Mountain. The trip takes about 10–14 days nonstop to appreciate its scenic highlights, many hikers do the trip in stages over more than one season.

Hikers will need a free wilderness permit for camping each night along the trail in one of 18 designated campsites. Reservations are recommended and can be made from April 15 through September 30. For information on weather and trip preparation ask for a free "Wilderness Trip Planner" by calling the Longmire Museum at (360) 569-2211x 3314 year-round, or the Wilderness Information Center at (360) 569-HIKE, late May through September. You may also visit the park website at www.nps.gov/mora/recreation.

The trail connects many photogenic subalpine meadows, including Indian Henry's Hunting Ground, Klapatche Park, Moraine Park, Berkeley Park, Summerland, and Indian Bar, forming a floral wreath that encircles The Mountain. Photographers capture "magic hour" reflections of The Mountain at Mirror, Aurora, Golden, Mowich, Mystic, and Reflection lakes. If flowers beckon, hikers opt for an alternate route through Spray Park. Big old trees and waterfalls on the Eastside Trail alternate route reward hikers avoiding wintry conditions at Panhandle Gap, the 6700-foot high point of the trail. Having completed the Wonderland Trail, we can agree with John Muir, "Wander here a whole summer if you can. Thousands of God's wild blessings will search you and soak you as if you were a sponge."

PAGE 52/53: Mount Rainier reflected in glacial tarn, evening in Spray Park. PHOTO ©CHARLES GURCHE

Vine maples and Douglas-fir, autumn.   PHOTO ©RON WARFIELD

Old growth of the Carbon River Rain Forest.   PHOTO ©FRED HIRSCHMANN

Monkeyflower lining Paradise River below Mazama Ridge.   PHOTO ©JOHN BARGER

WILD COMMUNITIES

The founders of Mount Rainier National Park recognized that The Mountain is an arctic island in a temperate sea of forest. The forest seemed endless in 1899, so park boundaries were drawn close to The Mountain's base. In less than 100 years, the old-growth forests that once extended to the shores of Puget Sound were clear-cut. Except in protected wilderness or in parks such as Mount Rainier, the old-growth forests are gone.

As the world grows more crowded, the forests and meadows of the park increase in value as scenic refuges for human seekers of wilderness solitude. Native resident/migrant animal species also depend more upon the park for their survival as habitat loss, fragmentation, and succession, along with predation and migration mortality, cause decline elsewhere.

The interplay of temperate climate and broad elevation range has resulted in various habitats for a marvelous diversity of plants and animals. Specialized communities have developed within the low-elevation old-growth forests of the river valleys, the dense forests of the montane slopes, the legendary subalpine parklands, and the rocky alpine zones. Arctic-alpine vegetation extends higher on Mount Rainier than any other Cascade volcano—nearly 12,000 feet. Large predators like the grizzly bear, lynx, wolf, and Chinook salmon are gone, but nearly all of the other animals, including 159 birds, 63 mammals, 16 amphibians, 5 reptiles, 18 native fishes, and myriad invertebrates still inhabit the park.

Employing a hands-off policy, the National Park Service monitors the natural processes that maintain this diverse ecosystem while The Mountain takes care of itself. Native species are well adapted to 20-foot-deep snowpacks, summer droughts, and a bevy of volcanic events, including glacial outburst floods, lahars, rockfalls, pyroclastic flows, pumice, and ashfalls. Fire, flood, insects and disease occasionally reset the successional clock in forest habitats. Between disturbances, plant and animal communities succeed each other or evolve from bare ground toward stable, self-reproducing climax conditions through time.

Trampling by hikers and climbers severely affected the

flower-filled meadows prior to 1970. To preserve the meadows while allowing visitors to enjoy their fragile beauty, the National Park Service has eliminated camping in this zone and restricted hiking to established trails. Park crews and volunteers have stabilized eroded areas and revegetated bare spots using native species. The flower meadows of Paradise, Sunrise, and Tipsoo lakes are recovering their luxuriance. By minimizing our own impacts on the floral landscape, we can assure that future flower lovers will enjoy the finest floral display this side of "Paradise."

WILDFLOWERS

Mount Rainier offers a wide variety of habitats suitable for wildflowers especially adapted to dense forests, subalpine parkland, or arctic/alpine zones. Spring arrives in April in the lower forest just as the snowpack in subalpine parklands and higher elevations reaches its greatest depth. Skunk cabbage raises hooded yellow spathes in marshy areas around Longmire and Carbon River. Vanilla-leaf grows in great masses of three-parted leaves around the bases of trees. Western trillium, calypso orchid, and bunchberry make individual displays worth a search in May and June. In small openings, twinflower forms mats of leathery leaves and sends up pairs of pinkish bell-shaped fragrant flowers. Salal and Oregon grape form thickets in drier soils while devil's club, salmonberry, and several huckleberries prefer moister sites. In late June, slender bog orchids, crimson columbine, goatsbeard, tall bluebell, yellow violet, and queen's cup lily join a number of heath family plants to brighten openings in mid-elevation forests.

Snowbanks linger into mid-July in subalpine meadows. Golden glacier lily pushes up around the edges of melting snowbanks and avalanche lily spreads a white carpet over spaces recently melted free. Cream-colored western anemone dots the lily fields. Shooting star, willow-herb, and yellow and pink Lewis monkey flowers crowd small rivulets of snowmelt. False hellebore, huckleberry, and mountain ash form thickets of vegetation within the meadows.

Only three weeks after glacier lily blooms, the shaggy seedheads of western anemone join a kaleidoscope of color. Masses of subalpine lupine spread a blue-violet tapestry as magenta paintbrush accents the white sea of Sitka valerian and American bistort. Then lavender fleabane and cascade aster join golden arnica and senecio. Brilliant pink cliff penstemon and blue-purple Davidson's penstemon brighten cliffs and talus slopes. Several species of lousewort, including Mount Rainier lousewort, are conspicuous among the meadow plants. Where new unstable ground is uncovered by glacial melt, Tolmie's saxifrage, mountain sorrel, and marsh marigold grow in wet areas among lush mosses. Luetkea and black sedge prefer drier sites. Well-drained pumice soils and drier climate in the northeastern parks favor

Vine maple and Spruce-Hemlock Forest.   PHOTO ©TERRY DONNELLY

Sub-alpine fir and mountain hemlock above Paradise.   PHOTO ©FRED HIRSCHMANN

Old growth in Grove of The Patriarchs.   PHOTO ©TIM FITZHARRIS

Pink spreading phlox.   PHOTO ©LARRY ULRICH

Mountain ash in autumn colors.   PHOTO ©JOHN MARSHALL

Bunchberry dogwood.   PHOTO ©JEFF D. NICHOLAS

bunchgrasses, sedges, and drought-resistant herbaceous plants, such as Gray's ligusticum and scarlet paintbrush. When violet mountain bog gentian joins white pearly everlasting, the huckleberry leaves have already begun their autumn color change.

Alpine heath communities of pink, white, and ivory heather form dense compact mats in response to nine-month snow-cover and moist soil. These heath communities have been trapping soil and growing continuously for more than 7000 years, making them some of Earth's oldest living things.

Near the upper limit of vegetation, plants must adapt to only a two-month snow-free growing season, constant winds, periods of dryness, and poorly developed soils. It's a tough habitat, where perennial plants grow as cushions or mats, leaves are insulated and protected by hairs, and roots reach deeply. Fellfield stones protect plants from winds and shelter roots from drought and erosion. Moss campion and alpine golden daisy add color to this extreme alpine habitat.

TREES

Mount Rainier lies west of the Cascade Range moisture divide, so it enjoys a temperate, maritime climate. July and August are comparatively dry, but a rainy season lasts from October through April. At higher elevations, snow accumulates from early November, building to 20-foot depths by early April. Several climatic zones exist in the forests around The Mountain because of its 12,700-foot elevational gradient. The Mountain is so massive that it creates its own rain (snow) shadow. This leaves the northeast side comparatively drier than the southwestern side. Topographic diversity, fires, avalanches, lahars, volcanic eruptions, insects, disease, soil development, and moisture availability add complexity to patterns of forest vegetation within the altitudinal life zones of the park.

Forests cover nearly 60 percent of the park. Three main life zones—Western Hemlock (Tsuga heterophylla), Pacific Silver Fir (Abies amabilis), and Mountain Hemlock (Tsuga mertensiana)—are characterized by a single dominant climax tree species. Zone boundaries are set primarily by elevation and temperature. Specific plant cover variation is determined by moisture (including snow), soil type, and length of time since major disturbance.

The Western Hemlock zone (about 1700–2800 feet in elevation) extends up the park's major river valleys. Large-girthed Douglas-firs grow in disturbed areas and stand out among the hemlocks. Superior seed germination and growth under shady conditions allow western hemlock to gradually replace Douglas-fir and dominate in mature forests. Shreddy-barked, buttress-based western redcedar grows in wet areas and valley floors. Sitka spruce grows in boggy sites in the Carbon River Valley while grand fir and western white pine occupy drier sites. Deciduous trees growing among the giant conifers provide contrasting colors in autumn. Bigleaf maple, red alder, black cottonwood and vine maple occupy valley bottoms, where sword ferns, devil's club, salal, salmonberry, and huckleberries make up a dense understory.

The Pacific Silver Fir zone (about 2500–4700 feet) extends through mid-elevations. Extremely shade tolerant silver fir outcompetes even western hemlock over time, so that pure climax stands develop after other species die out. Douglas-fir is present in disturbed areas. Cooler air and heavy snowpacks favor Alaska yellow-cedar and noble fir in moister areas and Engelmann spruce and lodgepole pine in well-drained sites. Short shrubs and herbs, such as huckleberries and beargrass, form an open understory.

The Mountain Hemlock zone (about 4500–6000 feet) grades into the open parkland environment of the subalpine meadows, reaching timberline at about 6000 feet. Mountain hemlock claims rocky ridges or grow in clumps on slopes that melt out early. Subalpine fir grows in richer soil or in areas where snowpacks linger. Subalpine fir forms clumps that spread when lower branches take root and send up new shoots in a process called layering. Whitebark pine forms clumps in meadows on The Mountain's northeast side. Alaska yellow-cedar grows in moister areas and Engelmann spruce occupies drier eastside slopes. The park's oldest tree, an Alaska yellow-cedar, has avoided fire, avalanche, and windthrow for 1200 years on the slopes above Ipsut Creek.

BIRDS

The park records 159 bird species that reside or visit seasonally. Year-round residents include ravens, gray jays, dark-eyed juncos, Clark's nutcrackers, chickadees, white-tailed ptarmigans, and gray-crowned rosy finches in the snow-covered subalpine zone.

At lower elevations, brown creepers and red-breasted nuthatches glean insects from bark crevices in the old-growth forest. They nest in loose bark or dead snags and move when weather or food availability dictates. Cheerful sounds of winter wrens echo through dense shrub layers throughout winter. Chestnut-backed chickadees nest in fur-lined holes in snags dug by woodpeckers.

When the snow cover melts from the lower forest in April, steam-whistle calls of varied thrushes proclaim spring. Hermit thrushes return from lowlands to forage on the ground for earthworms, insects, and berries. Flocks of pine siskins and golden-crowned kinglets populate the treetops and catch insects or snatch seeds and buds from branch tips. Pileated woodpeckers chop large squarish holes in snags for their nests. Red-shafted flickers find insects in the soil, but pileated woodpeckers prefer carpenter ants found in dead trees in the old-growth forest. Spotted owls eat

Western trillium.

Skunk cabbage blossom.

Western anemone seedheads.

Spotted owl.   PHOTO ©ART WOLFE

Mountain lion (cougar).   PHOTO ©TIM FITZHARRIS

White-tailed ptarmigan in winter plumage.   PHOTO ©ART WOLFE

primarily northern flying squirrels and nest in large hollow snags with good surrounding cover found only in the multi-aged canopy of old-growth forest. Marbled murrelets fly 50 to 100 miles inland from ocean feeding sites to nest exclusively in moss-covered upper branches of ancient trees.

Some birds that inhabit subalpine meadows in summer descend into the forest zone when snows accumulate. Blue grouse eat Douglas-fir needles all winter, then gorge on caterpillars, plant shoots, berries and buds in summer. Deep blue, black-crested Steller's jays rob food caches of other birds and eat anything available. Their call often mimics the scream of red-tailed hawks.

Larger size, flashy black-and-white wings and tail, and long bill separate Clark's nutcrackers from their corvid cousin, the gray jay. These aggressive birds pry seeds from conifer cones and store more than they eat. They prefer whitebark pine seeds, though blister rust disease is decimating this food source. Substitute food includes insects and anything a crow would eat. Gray jays eat conifer seeds, berries, insects, and meat when they find it. Their boldness reminds visitors that winter is livable for the well adapted.

Ravens eat seeds, rodents, insects, worms, eggs, young birds, carrion, and can even catch young snowshoe hares. Their guttural voice, watchful eye, and food cache memory connote great intelligence.

Gray-crowned rosy finches nest above timberline and forage on insects that collect on glaciers and snowbanks up to 11,000 feet on The Mountain. They also feed on seeds, white heather flowers, and saxifrage leaves around melting snow banks.

White-tailed ptarmigans, pipits, and horned larks forage on high-elevation snowfields for insects, spiders, and plant tidbits in summer. Ptarmigans survive winter on willow buds and crowberries. They molt to pure white plumage in winter and rely on camouflage to avoid the attention of predators. Feathers grow heavily on their legs and feet giving them snowshoes and insulation on the snow.

MAMMALS

More than 60 mammal species inhabit Mount Rainier National Park. The whistles and shrieks of hoary marmots announce the arrival of newcomers to subalpine meadows. These largest squirrel family members munch their way through the short summer season, then hibernate from September through May.

Snowshoe hares remain active on the snow, using white furry camouflage to avoid red fox and bobcat predators. Hares eat conifer buds and shrub bark and sleep in shallow depressions under shrubs. Heather voles and pocket gophers remain active beneath the snow, subsisting on meadow plant shoots. Pikas, the guinea pig-sized relatives of rabbits, occupy talus slopes and rocky outcrops, where they eat their way through haystacks of meadow vegetation stored under large rocks. Their nasal "eenk" calls alert other pikas to predators. Deer mice are the most abundant prey species for pine martens, short- and long-tailed weasels, and mink. Both weasels turn white in winter and remain active upon the snow. Pine martens search the tree canopy for Douglas squirrels and northern flying squirrels in summer then forage on the ground in winter for voles and hares.

All of Mount Rainier's bats feed on abundant nocturnal flying insects, and then roost in tree cavities and well-shaded branches in daytime. When insects wane, bats hibernate. Shrews remain active under snow, searching the forest floor for worms, grubs, and insect larvae.

Noisy Douglas squirrels clip and cache volumes of cones from conifers. Northern flying squirrels eat truffles (underground fungi fruiting bodies) in summer and nibble horsehair lichen in winter. Golden-mantled ground squirrels fatten grossly on seeds in autumn and hibernate for months. Chipmunks store seeds, insects, and fungi and rely on stored food in winter.

Coyotes prey on small rodents, berries, hares, and winter-killed deer or elk. Red foxes consume mice and squirrels, insects, hares, fruit, seeds, and eggs. Their white-tipped tail identifies them as a red fox, though their body fur may be black, silver, or reddish brown with black legs.

Black bears (including brown and cinnamon color phases) eat anything that is handy—lush meadow vegetation, carrion, small mammals, grubs or insect nests, tree cambium, berries, and fish. In fall, subalpine meadows become bear berry buffets before the bears make hibernation dens at lower elevations.

Cougars, or mountain lions, prey on grasshoppers, mice, porcupines, and other mammals all the way up to elk. Ranging from lower forest to subalpine meadows, cougars are the major predator of deer.

Black-tailed deer (a subspecies of mule deer) fatten up on herbaceous plants in summer meadows, but move to river bottoms near the park boundary in winter to browse on shrubs, lichens, and mushrooms. Elk, extirpated from the Cascades before the park was established, were reintroduced in the early 20th century. Browsing by herds of elk has caused soil and vegetation damage in eastern valleys and meadows.

Mountain goats, masters of Mount Rainier's montane terrain, rely on their hard, rubbery hoof pads to move freely across cliffs in search of lichens, mosses, meadow grasses, and flowers. Look for these alpine residents at Mildred Point, Burroughs Mountain, or Mount Fremont.

Pika.   PHOTO ©ART WOLFE

Hoary marmot.   PHOTO ©JOHN BARGER

Mountain goat.   PHOTO ©CRAIG BLACKLOCK/LARRY ULRICH STOCK

PAGE 60/61: Sunrise reflections at Reflection Lakes. PHOTO ©CHARLES GURCHE

IN CASE OF EMERGENCY
Emergency & Medical
 Call 911
 —or—
Mount Rainier National Park
 (360) 569-2211

MORE INFORMATION
Mount Rainier National Park
 55210 238th Avenue East
 Ashford, WA 98304
 E-mail: MORAInfo@nps.gov
 (360) 569-2211
 (360) 569-2177 (TDD)
 www.nps.gov/mora
Northwest Interpretive Association
 (360) 569-2211x3320
 www.nwpubliclands.com
Washington's National Park Fund
 (206) 770-0627
 www.wnpf.org
Current Road Conditions
 (800) 695-ROAD (Dept. of Trans.)
 (360) 569-2211 (NPS)

PARK LODGING
Mount Rainier Guest Services
 PO Box 108
 Ashford, WA 98304
 (360) 569-2275
 www.guestservices.com/rainier

LODGING OUTSIDE THE PARK
Mount Rainier Visitor Association
 PO Box 214
 Ashford, WA 98304
 (877) 617-9950 (toll-free)
 www.mt-rainier.com/contact.htm

PARK CAMPING
National Park Service
 (Summer only)
 (800) 365-CAMP
 www.nps.gov/mora/recreation/camping.htm
Wilderness Permits
 Wilderness Reservations Office
 Mount Rainier National Park
 55210 238th Avenue East
 Ashford, WA 98304
 www.nps.gov/mora/recreation/wic.htm

OTHER REGIONAL SITES
Ebey's Landing National Historical Site
 PO Box 774
 162 Cemetery Road
 Coupeville, WA 98239
 (360) 678-6084
 www.nps.gov/ebla
Fort Vancouver National Historic Site
 612 E. Reserve Street
 Vancouver, WA 98661
 (360) 696-7655x10
 www.nps.gov/fova

Klondike Gold Rush National Historical Park
 (Seattle Unit)
 319 Second Street South
 Seattle, WA 98104
 (206) 220-4240
 www.nps.gov/klse
Lake Chelan National Recreation Area
 c/o North Cascades National Park
 810 State Route 20

 Sedro-Woolley, WA 98284
 (360) 856-5700
 www.nps.gov/lach
Lake Roosevelt National Recreation Area
 1008 Crest Drive
 Coulee Dam, WA 99116
 (509) 633-9441
 www.nps.gov/laro
North Cascades National Park
 810 State Route 20
 Sedro-Woolley, WA 98284
 (360) 856-5700
 www.nps.gov/noca
Olympic National Park
 600 East Park Avenue
 Port Angeles, WA 98362
 (360) 565-3130
 www.nps.gov/olym

Ross Lake National Recreation Area
 c/o North Cascades National Park
 810 State Route 20
 Sedro-Woolley, WA 98284
 (360) 856-7500
 www.nps.gov/rola
San Juan Island National Historical Park
 PO Box 429
 Friday Harbor, WA 98250
 (360) 378-2902
 www.nps.gov/sajh
Whitman Mission National Historic Site
 328 Whitman Mission Road
 Walla Walla, WA 99362
 (509) 522-6357
 www.nps.gov/whmi

NATIONAL FOREST INFORMATION
Columbia River Gorge National Scenic Area
 902 Wasco Street, Suite 200
 Hood River, OR 97031
 (541) 386-2333
 www.fs.fed.us/r6/columbia/forest
Colville National Forest
 765 South Main Street
 Colville, WA 99114
 (509) 684-7000
 www.fs.fed.us/r6/colville
Gifford Pinchot National Forest
 10600 NE 51st Circle
 Vancouver, WA 98682
 (360) 891-5000
 www.fs.fed.us/gpnf
Mount Baker–Snoqualmie National Forest
 21905 64th Avenue W
 Mountlake Terrace, WA 98043
 (425) 775-9702
 www.fs.fed.us/r6/mbs
Mount Hood National Forest
 16400 Champion Way
 Sandy, OR 97055
 (503) 668-1700
 www.fs.fed.us/r6/mthood
Mount St. Helens National Volcanic Monument
 Monument Headquarters
 42218 NE Yale Bridge Road
 Amboy, WA 98601
 (360) 449-7800
 —or—
Mount St. Helens Visitor Center
 3029 Spirit Lake Highway
 Castle Rock, WA 98611
 (360) 274-0962
Okanagan National Forest
 215 Melody Lane
 Wenatchee, WA 98801
 (509) 664-9200
 www.fs.fed.us/r6/oka
Wenatchee National Forest
 215 Melody Lane
 Wenatchee, WA 98801
 (509) 664-9200
 www.fs.fed.us/r6/wenatchee

ABOVE: Avalanche lilies and pond in Indian Henrys Hunting Ground. PHOTO ©JOHN MARSHALL   **OPPOSITE:** Mount Rainier and Carbon Glacier seen from Moraine Park. PHOTO ©LARRY ULRICH

PRODUCTION CREDITS

Publisher: Jeff D. Nicholas
Author: Ron Warfield
Editor: Nicky Leach
Illustrations: Darlece Cleveland
Printing Coordination: Sung In Printing America

ISBN 10: 1-58071-067-0 (Paper)
ISBN 13: 978-1-58071-067-1 (Paper)
©2007 Panorama International Productions, Inc.

Printed in the Republic of South Korea.
First printing, Spring 2007.

SIERRA PRESS

4988 Gold Leaf Drive, Mariposa, CA 95338
(209) 966-5071, 966-5073 (Fax)
e-mail: siepress@sti.net

SIERRA PRESS
VISIT OUR WEBSITE AT:
www.NationalParksUSA.com

OPPOSITE
Mount Rainier reflected in glacial tarn, evening in Moraine Park. PHOTO ©ALAN MAJCHROWICZ
BELOW
Pinnacle Peak of the Tatoosh Range.
PHOTO ©RON WARFIELD